Immigration Stories

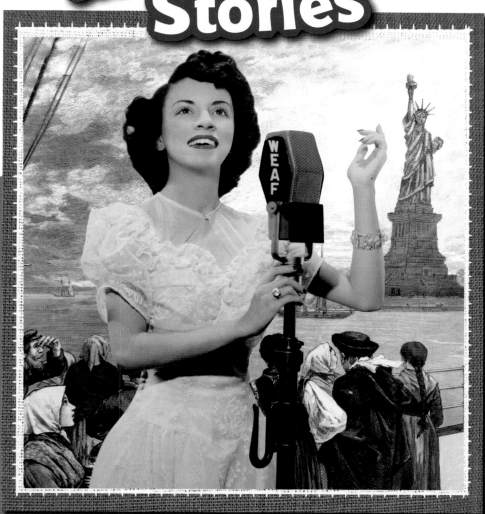

Marcus McArthur, Ph.D.

Consultants

Shelley Scudder
Gifted Education Teacher
Broward County Schools

Caryn Williams, M.S.Ed.
Madison County Schools
Huntsville, AL

Publishing Credits

Conni Medina, M.A.Ed., *Managing Editor*
Lee Aucoin, *Creative Director*
Torrey Maloof, *Editor*
Marissa Rodriguez, *Designer*
Stephanie Reid, *Photo Editor*
Rachelle Cracchiolo, M.S.Ed., *Publisher*

Image Credits: Cover, pp. 1, 16, 18- 19, 20 Michelle Arias; pp. 9, 6 Berkeley Architectural Heritage Association; pp. 10–11 Bridgeman; p. 15 Famous Records courtesy of the Judica Sound Archives; pp. 8–9, 17, 21 Getty Images; p. 12 The Granger Collection; p. 4 The Library of Congress [LC-DIG-ggbain-30546]; p. 26–27 Stephanie Reid/The Library of Congress [LC-USZC2-1255]; pp. 11, 32 Courtesy of the Milken Archive; p. 13 National Parks; pp. 6–7, 23–25, 28 Newscom; All other images from Shutterstock.

Teacher Created Materials

5301 Oceanus Drive
Huntington Beach, CA 92649-1030
http://www.tcmpub.com
ISBN 978-1-4333-6998-8
© 2014 Teacher Created Materials, Inc.

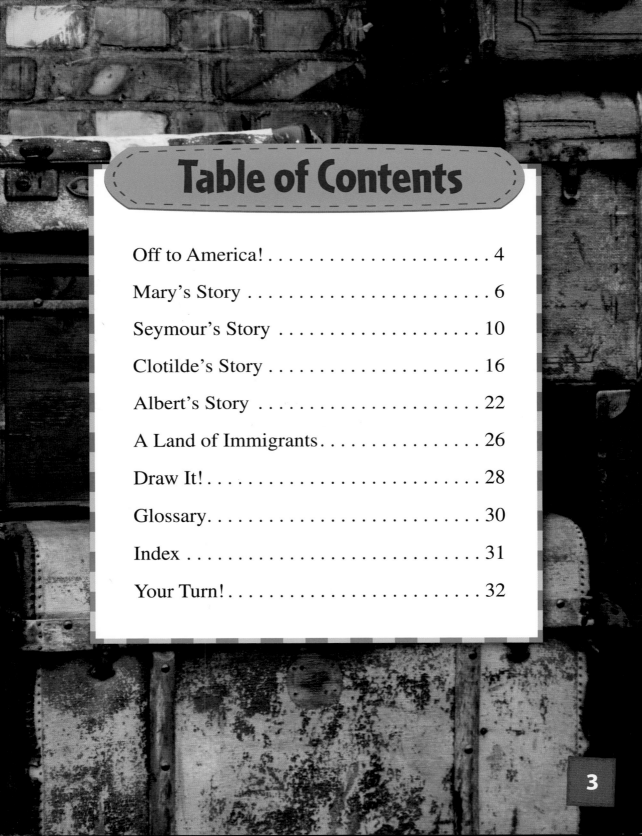

Table of Contents

These immigrants step onto American land for the first time.

Off to America!

There are many **immigrants** (IM-i-gruhntz) in America. Immigrants are people who move to a new country to live there. Each immigrant has a story to tell. They tell stories about where they came from. They tell stories about their lives in America.

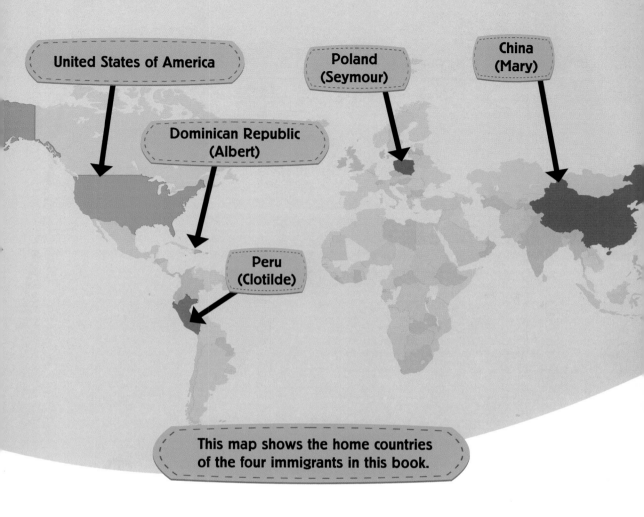

This map shows the home countries of the four immigrants in this book.

In this book, you will read the stories of four immigrants. Their names are Seymour (SEE-mohr), Mary, Clotilde (klo-TEEL-deh), and Albert.

Mary's Story

Mary was born in China in 1857. She was an **orphan** (OR-fuhn). Orphans do not have parents to raise them.

This is Mary as an adult with her husband.

When Mary was 11 years old, her life changed. An American brought her to live in San Francisco, California. She lived in a house with other orphans. She learned to speak English there.

Angel Island

Many Chinese immigrants came to America through Angel Island in San Francisco. It was an **immigration** station.

Angel Island

When Mary was 18 years old, she married Joseph Tape. He was an immigrant from China, too. Mary and Joseph had four kids. They raised their kids in San Francisco.

These are Chinese students in San Francisco in 1920.

Back then, Chinese kids were not allowed to go to the same schools as white kids. In 1885, Mary fought hard to change this **law**. Other people joined Mary's fight. But the law was not changed until 1947.

Tale of Tape

Joseph Tape's name had been Chew Diep (DEE-ehp). He wanted an American name. So he changed *Chew* to *Joe* and *Diep* to *Tape*.

This is Joseph and Mary in 1930.

Seymour's Story

Seymour Rechtzeit (RECK-zayt) was a young boy living in Poland. He loved to sing. He was very good at it. It was not long before Seymour became famous.

Seymour grew up in a Polish village like this one.

Seymour sang in many concerts. People in Poland called him *wunderkind* (VOON-der-kind). This means "wonder child." Seymour was only four years old!

This poster shows Seymour as a star in Poland.

Seymour's parents thought he could be a bigger star in America. In 1920, Seymour and his father left Poland for America. It was a long and very cold boat trip.

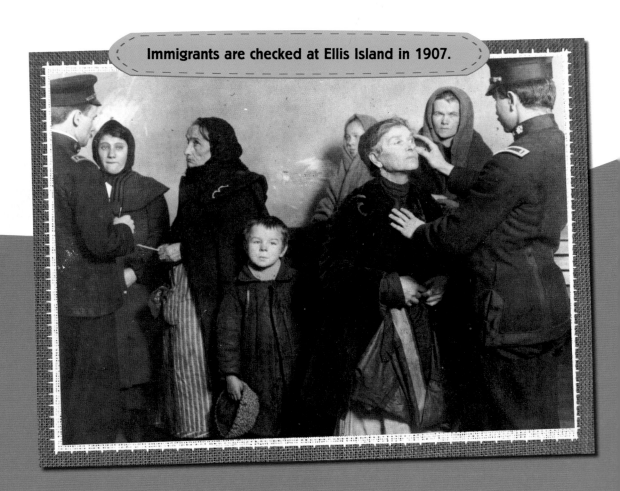

Immigrants are checked at Ellis Island in 1907.

They arrived at Ellis Island. They were checked to make sure they were healthy. If immigrants were sick, they could not enter the country. Seymour was sick. He had to stay at Ellis Island until he was well.

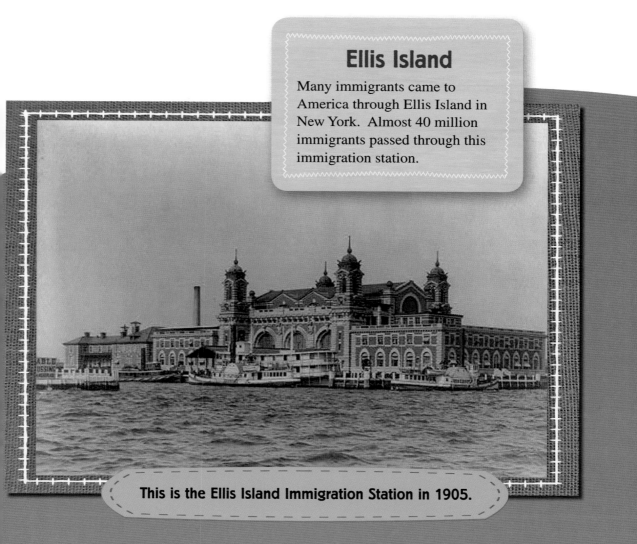

Ellis Island

Many immigrants came to America through Ellis Island in New York. Almost 40 million immigrants passed through this immigration station.

This is the Ellis Island Immigration Station in 1905.

Seymour got better. He soon became a star in America. He made enough money to bring the rest of his family over from Poland. But a new law set **quotas** (KWOH-tuhz), or limits, on immigration. This meant that Seymour's family could not come to America.

Calvin Coolidge was president when Seymour sang.

One day, Seymour sang for the president of the
United States. President Coolidge liked Seymour's song.
He helped bring Seymour's family to America!

Seymour made records as an adult. This
is the front and back of one of his records.

Clotilde Arias

Clotilde's Story

Clotilde Arias grew up in Peru. She loved music as a young girl. She liked writing poems and songs, too. She wanted to go to school to learn more about music. But there were not many music schools in Peru.

Clotilde went to a music school like this one.

Clotilde knew there were more music schools in America. So in 1923, she moved to New York City.

Clotilde was excited to study music. But her family had a hard time making money. She had to give up her studies. She got a job as a nurse to help her family.

Clotilde (far right) poses with other nurses.

Clotilde was sad. But she did not give up on her dream. She worked hard at many jobs. She even wrote songs to sell things on the radio.

Clotilde sings a song on the radio.

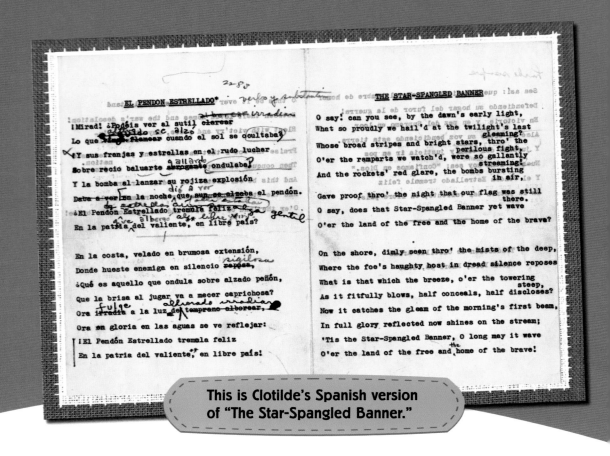

This is Clotilde's Spanish version of "The Star-Spangled Banner."

In 1945, Clotilde had a chance to do something big. She was asked to write a Spanish version of "The Star-Spangled Banner." This is the national **anthem**. It is America's song.

This woman is singing Clotilde's anthem today.

This was a big **honor**. Clotilde was happy to do it. Now, more people could sing the song. Many immigrants have sung Clotilde's song. Many still sing it.

Albert's Story

Albert Pujols grew up in the Dominican Republic. He loved to play baseball. He played baseball after school. He would play until it was too dark to see the ball.

This is a baseball, a glove, and a bat.

But Albert's grandmother wanted a better life for him. She thought Albert would have more chances to **succeed** (suhk-SEED) in America. In 1996, Albert's family moved to Missouri (mi-ZOOR-ee).

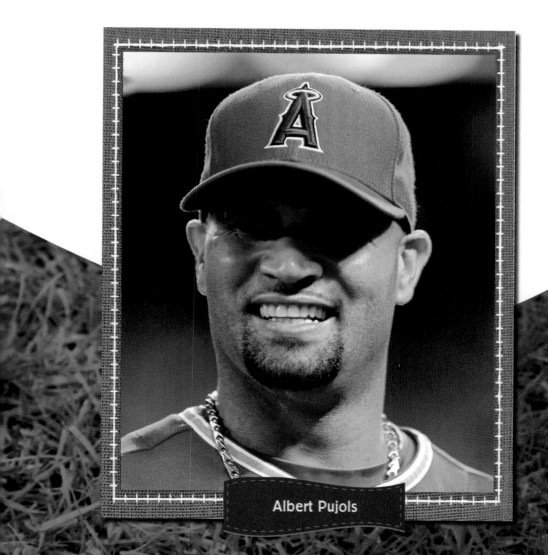

Albert Pujols

Albert became a star on his high school baseball team. People saw that he was good. In 2001, the St. Louis Cardinals asked him to join the team.

Albert hits a home run in 2011.

Albert was now a **professional** baseball player. He got paid to play baseball. He became one of the best players in history. Albert's dream came true.

Playing for the Angels

In 2012, Albert started playing baseball with the Angels. The Angels are a team in California.

Albert teaches kids in the Dominican Republic how to play baseball.

A Land of Immigrants

America is a land of immigrants. They come to America from different countries around the world. They move here for different reasons.

These boys came to America from another country.

Immigrants bring their talents and ideas. They do great things for America. They help make America a great country.

Immigrants see the Statue of Liberty in New York City for the first time.

Draw It!

Imagine you are one of the immigrants in this book. How would you feel about your journey to America? Draw a picture to show your feelings.

These immigrants are waving American flags.

This girl is drawing a picture of an immigrant.

Glossary

anthem—a formal song of loyalty, praise, or happiness

honor—respect that is given to someone who is admired

immigrants—people who move to another country to live there

immigration—when people move to another country to live there

law—a rule made by the government

orphan—a child who does not have parents

professional—doing a job for money

quotas—limits

succeed—to do what you are trying to do

Index

Your Turn!

A Special Song

Seymour sang a song for the president. The words of the song made the president want to help Seymour's family. Write a special song about immigration. Set the song to a tune you already know.

Immigration Stories

Immigrants move to America for many reasons. Each of them has a story to tell. Immigrants help make America a great country.

History

Houghton Mifflin Harcourt

Immigration

RL: 2.4

ISBN-13: 978-1-4333-6998-8

50000

9 781433 369988

TCM 17998